DRAWING

PUPPIES, CHICKS,

AND OTHER BABY ANIMALS

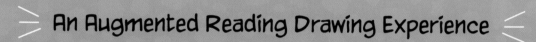

An Augmented Reading Drawing Experience

BY CLARA CELLA

ILLUSTRATED BY SYDNEY HANSON

CAPSTONE PRESS
a capstone imprint

Dabble Lab Books are published by Capstone Press,
1710 Roe Crest Drive, North Mankato, Minnesota 56003
www.mycapstone.com

Library of Congress Cataloging-in-Publication data is available
on the Library of Congress website.
ISBN: 978-1-5435-3189-3 (library binding)
ISBN: 978-1-5435-4238-7 (eBook PDF)

Summary: Easy-to-follow instructions and special 4D components show
aspiring artists how to draw puppies, chicks, kittens, and other cuddle-
worthy baby animals step-by-step. Projects increase in difficulty to build
drawing skills and instill confidence. Readers can download the Capstone
4D app for an augmented reality experience that extends learning beyond
the printed page with artist video tutorials and other bonus content.

Editorial Credits
Jill Kalz, editor; Aruna Rangarajan, designer;
Kathy McColley, production specialist

Photo Credits
Capstone Studio: Karon Dubke, 31 (pouch); Shutterstock:
Jamen Percy, 5 (pencils and scribbles), Lifestyle Graphic (sheet
of paper), cover and throughout, Mega Pixel, 5 (erasers and pencil
sharpener), Oksana Telesheva (spotted background), cover and
throughout, Ruslan Ivantsov, 5 (graphite pencil), timquo, 5 (felt marker)

Printed in the United States of America.
PA017

TABLE OF CONTENTS

HELLO, ARTIST!

QUESTION: Could this book be any cuter?

ANSWER: No! Ten of the sweetest baby animals around have crawled, hopped, and skipped onto these pages. And they've done so for one reason—to have their portraits drawn by you!

 SO LET'S GET STARTED:

Easier projects, such as the chick, are toward the front of the book. More challenging projects are toward the back. Just follow the steps and practice, practice, practice. If you need some help, scan the star targets to pop up your 4D instructor. Soon you'll be turning blank sheets of paper into a big stack of "Aww"!

Tools and Supplies

Before you begin your drawing projects,
gather the following tools and supplies:

PAPER

Any type of blank, unlined paper will do.

PENCILS

Pencils are the easiest to use.
Make sure you have plenty of them.

SHARPENER

You'll need clean lines, so keep
a pencil sharpener close by.

ERASER

Pencil erasers wear out very quickly.
Get a rubber or kneaded eraser.

DARK PEN/MARKER

When your drawing is finished, you can
trace over it with a black ink pen or a thin
felt-tip marker. The dark lines will really
make your work pop.

COLORED PENCILS

If you decide to color your drawings,
colored pencils usually work best.

CHICK

Look at that round, fluffy body and that tiny beak! Cute, right? Well, not everyone thinks so. Some people have a very real fear of chickens. The rare condition is called *alektorophobia* (ah-LEK-tohr-oh-FOH-be-ah). But don't worry. The chick you draw will *not* hurt you. Promise!

STEP 1

STEP 2

STEP 3

STEP 4

Try drawing a brood (group) of four or more little chicks.

STEP 5

TURTLE HATCHLING

"Big things come in small packages." Green sea turtle hatchlings are proof that this saying is true. They're about as long as your pinky finger when they start their lives in the ocean. But then they grow! Most adults measure 3 feet (91 centimeters) long and weigh more than 300 pounds (136 kilograms).

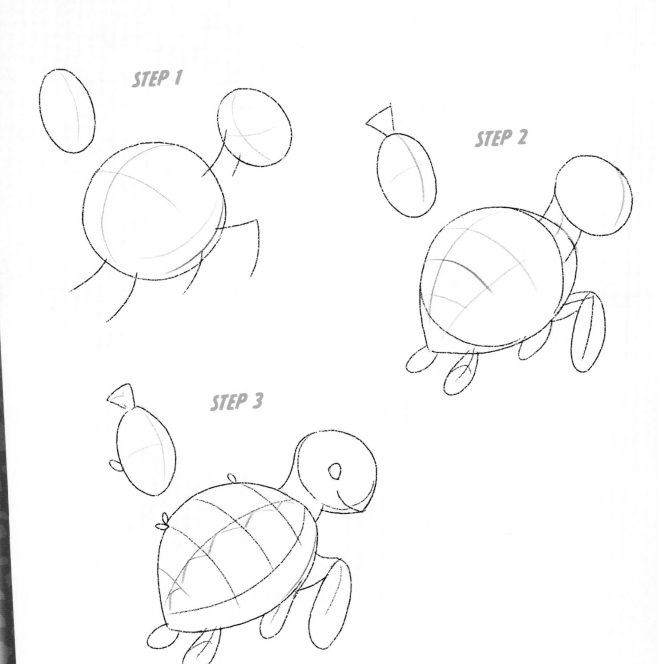

STEP 1

STEP 2

STEP 3

STEP 4

Once you've drawn this hatchling, draw another one with a wild pattern on its shell. Try squiggles, flowers, or stars.

STEP 5

BUNNY

For their first few weeks of life, bunnies drink milk from their mother. After that, they eat solid foods. While rabbits *do* eat carrots, they also eat grasses, clover, seeds, roots, buds, tree bark, and garden veggies. Rabbits are herbivores—animals that eat only plants.

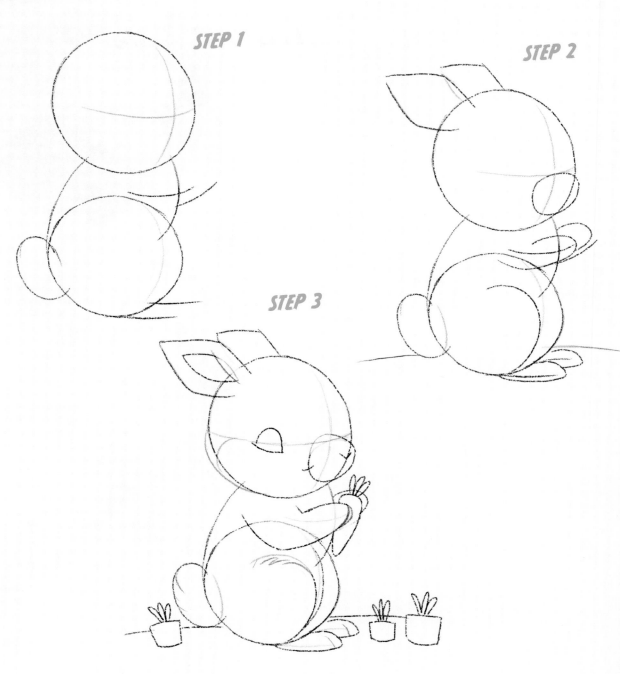

STEP 1

STEP 2

STEP 3

STEP 4

Draw a garden around your bunny, filled with leafy vegetables.

STEP 5

PANDA CUB

Why are giant pandas black and white? No one knows for sure. Some people think the colors help the animals hide. The black ears, eyes, nose, legs, and shoulders blend in with forest shadows. Other people think the markings are a way for pandas to know who's a panda and who's not!

STEP 1

STEP 2

STEP 3

STEP 4

Pandas usually sit upright when they eat, like a person. Try drawing a panda cub chewing on a thick stem of bamboo.

STEP 5

See the horn on this calf? It gave rhinos their name! "Rhinoceros" comes from two ancient words meaning "nose horn." The horn is made of keratin—a material also found in fingernails, hair, claws, and hooves. Javan and Indian rhinos have one horn. Three other rhino species have two.

STEP 1

STEP 2

STEP 3

STEP 4

STEP 5

After drawing
your rhino calf,
draw another one
splashing in
a watering hole.

DONKEY FOAL

Like many animals, male and female donkeys have different names. Males are jacks. Females are jennies or jennets. In the wild, donkey herds usually have just one jack and a number of jennies. Donkeys like living in groups, but they may change herds from time to time.

STEP 1

STEP 2

STEP 3

STEP 4

Donkeys are often used as pack animals. Try drawing a cart full of flowers for your donkey to pull.

STEP 5

More than 75 million pet dogs live in the United States. And they all started life the same way—as puppies! Newborn puppies can't see or hear for the first 10 days or so. They have no teeth. They spend nearly all day sleeping. But before long, they're ready to play!

STEP 1

STEP 2

STEP 3

STEP 4

Draw a leash on your puppy—and you, walking alongside.

STEP 5

ELEPHANT CALF

Big-time cute! At birth, baby African elephants weigh an average of 250 pounds (113 kg). That's about the same weight as a refrigerator! Calves are not only able to stand within minutes of being born, but they can also walk after an hour or two.

STEP 1

STEP 2

STEP 3

STEP 4

STEP 5

Try drawing your elephant calf's mother. Make her tall enough so her baby can stand beneath her.

PIGLET

Shocking news: Pigs are some of the cleanest animals in the world! But wait, you say. *Don't they roll around in mud?* They do, but they roll in mud to cool off, not because they love getting dirty. Pigs can't sweat well. Wallowing in cool water or mud keeps them from overheating.

STEP 1

STEP 2

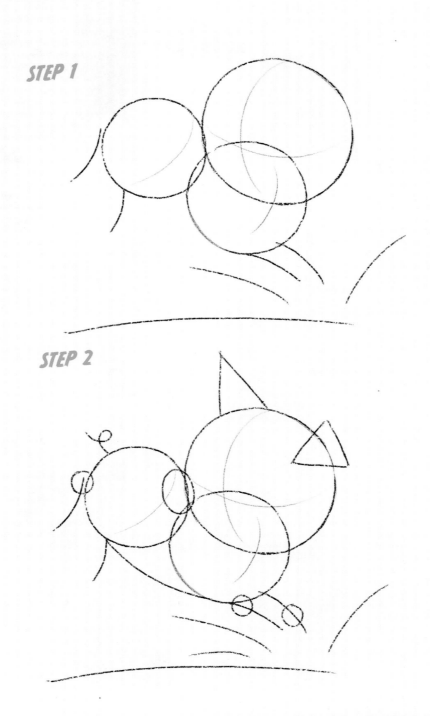

STEP 3

STEP 4

STEP 5

CONTINUED...

STEP 6

STEP 7

Keep your piglet cool! Draw it playing in a big, sloppy pool of mud.

STEP 8

CHEETAH CUB

Most of the world's wild cheetahs live on open grasslands in Africa. Their yellow coloring helps them blend in with the grasses. Patterns of black spots look like shadows. This camouflage allows adult cats to sneak up on prey. It also keeps cubs safe from predators such as lions and hyenas.

STEP 1

STEP 2

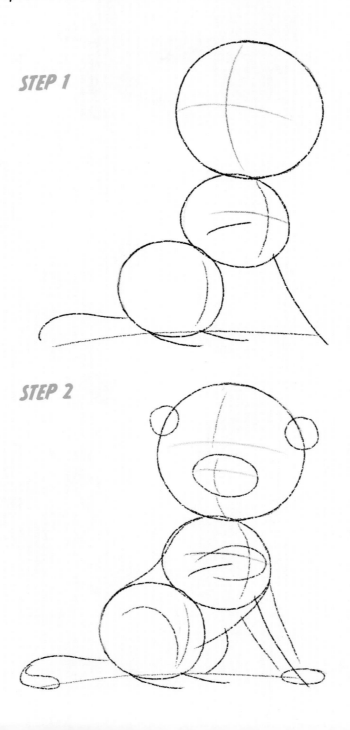

STEP 3

STEP 4

STEP 5

CONTINUED...

STEP 6

STEP 7

Try drawing your cheetah cub's mother. Keep her body lean and her legs long.

STEP 8

CRAFT IT UP!

CONGRATULATIONS! You finished all the projects. Now you've got pages and pages of drawings. Let's take one of those drawings and do something with it. Craft it up!

IRON-ON ANIMALS

WHAT YOU NEED:

- → a computer, with a scanner and printer
- → printable iron-on paper
- → scissors
- → a light-colored canvas pouch or book bag
- → an adult
- → an iron

STEP 1 Scan your drawing into the computer.

STEP 2 Load the printer with iron-on paper and print the image. *Note: Your drawing will transfer to the bag or pouch in reverse when you iron it later. So, if you want your finished product to look exactly like your drawing, you must flip the image before printing it.*

STEP 3 Cut out the image. Leave little or no edge around it.

STEP 4 Position the image, face down, on the canvas. Have an adult help you transfer the image, following the ironing instructions on the iron-on paper package.

STEP 5 Peel off the backing and show off your art!

READ MORE

Colich, Abby. *Drawing Wild Animals.* North Mankato, Minn.: Capstone Press, 2015.

Cuddy, Robbin. *Learn to Draw Dogs & Puppies: Step-by-Step Instructions for More Than 25 Different Breeds.* Irvine, Calif.: Walter Foster Publishing, 2015.

Hart, Christopher. *Drawing Cartoons from Numbers: Create Fun Characters from 1 to 1001. Drawing Shape by Shape Series.* New York: Drawing with Christopher Hart, 2018.

INTERNET SITES

Use FactHound to find Internet sites related to this book:

Visit *www.facthound.com*

Just type in 9781543531893 and go.

MAKERSPACE TIPS

Download tips and tricks for using this book and others in a library makerspace.

Visit *www.capstonepub.com/dabblelabresources*